WHO BUILT THAT?

SKYSCRAPERS

WHO BUILT THAT?

**An Introduction
to Skyscrapers
and Their Architects**

Didier Cornille

Princeton Architectural Press · New York

INTRODUCTION

Ever since the Tower of Babel in the Bible, humans have built soaring tall structures. With the development of iron architecture, we've been able to construct higher and higher buildings, such as the Eiffel Tower.

Skyscrapers were first developed in American cities in the late 1800s, but today they're found all over the world.

This book teaches you about the towers and skyscrapers that have captured so many architects' imaginations. You'll see how they are designed to be tall and lightweight, but also solid and capable of withstanding the forces of the wind and earth. And, most of all, you'll discover their beauty. Perhaps you'll visit or even live in one of these buildings someday.

CONTENTS

1889
THE EIFFEL TOWER

GUSTAVE EIFFEL

A TOWER MADE ONLY OF IRON

1,063 FEET (324 METERS)

Engineer Gustave Eiffel (1832–1923) specialized in metal construction and managed several work sites, including the railway bridge in Bordeaux, France. In 1867 he established his own company in Levallois-Perret, near Paris, France, and became known for his bold projects.

He designed some spectacular bridges,…

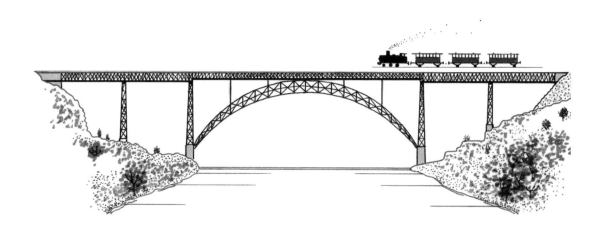

such as this one in Porto, Portugal (1877)…

and this one in Garabit, France (1884).

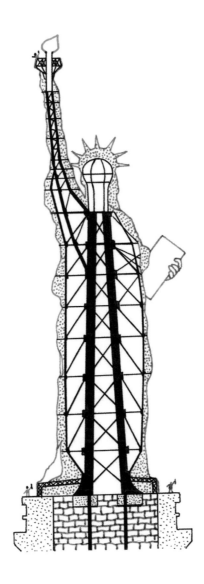

He also invented the giant framework for Frédéric Auguste Bartholdi's Statue of Liberty, which was installed in New York City in 1886.

According to Eiffel, iron was the material of the future. Lighter than brick or stone, it is both strong and flexible, allowing for large structures to be made out of crisscrossing solid iron beams.

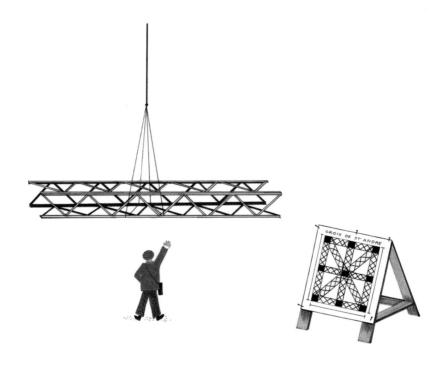

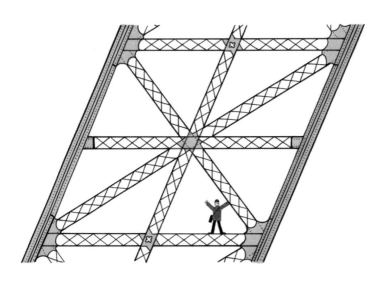

For the 1889 World's Fair, held in Paris, the engineer came up with a new idea, which would become the highlight of the fair: a 1,063-foot-tall (324-meter) tower of iron, built by the duo Émile Nouguier and Maurice Koechlin.

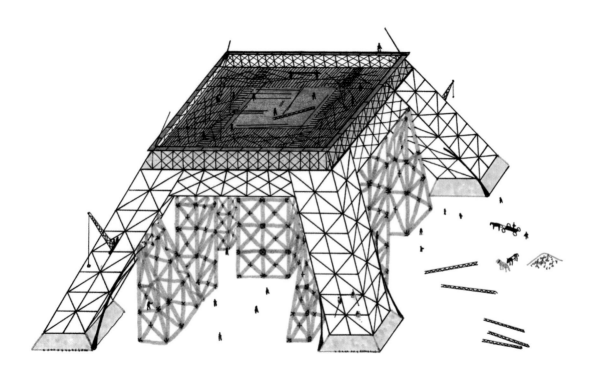

Anchored on four spread feet, this immense pylon becomes slimmer as it rises, as if it were designed by the wind. The four pillars come together in a shape that resembles a giant stool.

Higher up, the pillars join together in a single column made out of iron braces that continue to the very top.

The tower was expected to be torn down two decades after the fair. Yet, although it was criticized by many, the structure turned out to be very useful for the city, with an antenna installed at the top for radio transmissions. Today both radio and television stations use the tower as an antenna.

The Eiffel Tower soon became the symbol of Paris.

Eiffel used the tower to conduct research, studying the force of the wind at its summit and designing a testing device to measure gravity.

He had plans for making a flight simulator on a cable, but these were never carried out.

He also set up a wind tunnel near the tower.

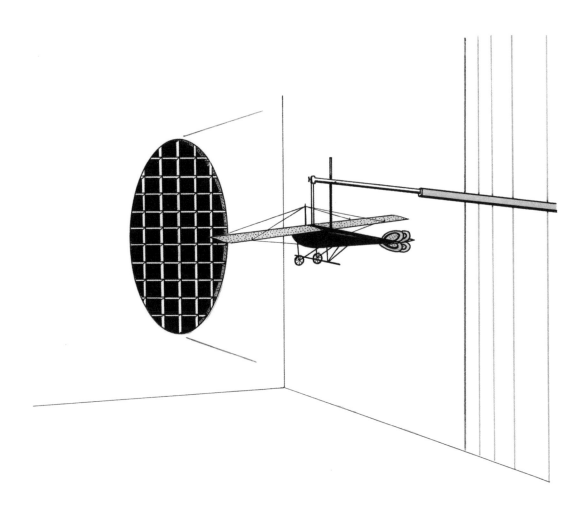

The pioneers of aviation tested their models there.

1895
THE PRUDENTIAL (GUARANTY) BUILDING

LOUIS SULLIVAN

AN ARTISTIC SKYSCRAPER

167 FEET (51 METERS)

Louis Sullivan (1856–1924) studied architecture in Boston, Massachusetts, then enrolled at the School of Fine Arts (l'École des Beaux-Arts) in Paris. After his return to the United States, he moved to Chicago, Illinois, which was in the process of rebuilding after the Great Chicago Fire of 1871. For the first time in the history of building, the use of light steel frames permitted the construction of very tall buildings with elevators (which were invented in 1853)—the first skyscrapers.

The Guaranty Building's sponsor, Hascal L. Taylor, wanted a prestigious, avant-garde (new and experimental) office building to attract businessmen to Buffalo, New York, and hired Sullivan to design it. The architect responded by constructing one of America's finest early skyscrapers.

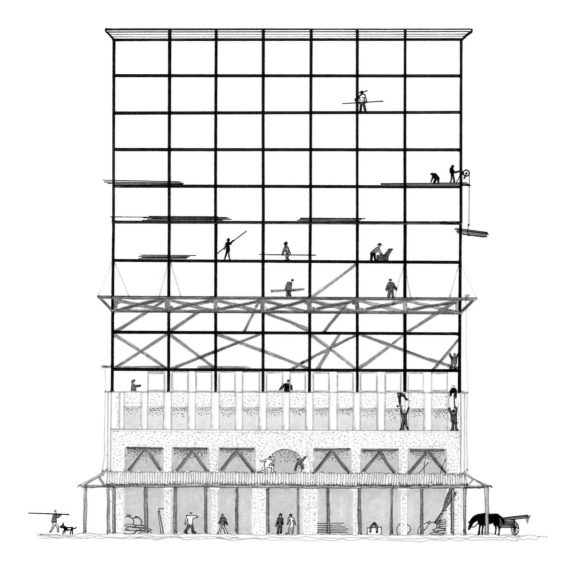

Sullivan understood that the modern city needed spaces dedicated to business and office work. Inspired by natural organisms, he designed buildings that responded to these functions with an adequate form.

Covered in terra cotta,* the facade† is made up of three different parts stacked on top of each other, not including the basement.

* A type of clay used to make pottery or building tiles
† One of the sides of a building (usually its front)

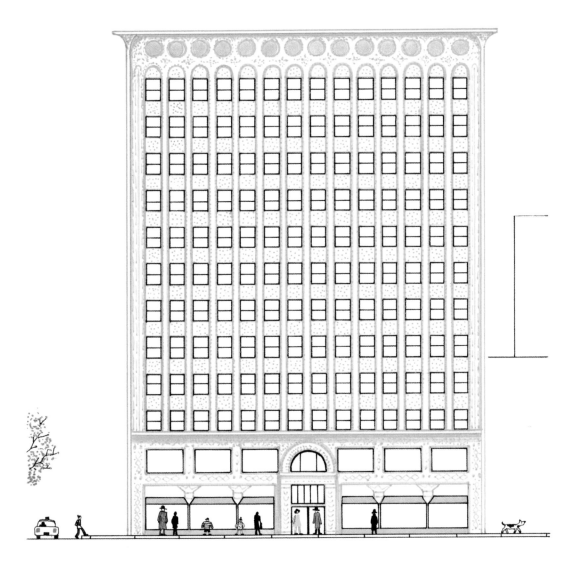

The ground floor features monumental doors that open up to shops. Next comes a stack of office floors. The top floor is crowned with Egyptian molding.‡

‡ A strip of patterned material used to decorate a building

Sullivan worked on a variety of other buildings.

He designed the Walker Warehouse (1889) in Chicago together
with his associate, the German-born engineer and architect Dankmar
Adler. This building no longer exists.

The Carson, Pirie, Scott & Company Building (1899) in Chicago was a large department store.

1930
THE CHRYSLER BUILDING

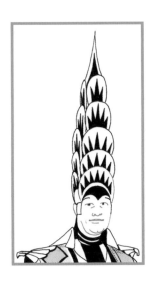

WILLIAM VAN ALEN

A CELEBRATION OF THE AUTOMOBILE

1,046 FEET (319 METERS)

After studying architecture at Pratt Institute in Brooklyn, New York, William Van Alen (1883–1954) moved to Paris, where he studied with Victor Laloux, the architect of the Parisian train station the Gare d'Orsay. In 1927, back in New York, he began working on a monumental dome-topped building. The automobile manufacturer Walter Chrysler had asked him to design the tallest skyscraper in the world to promote his business.

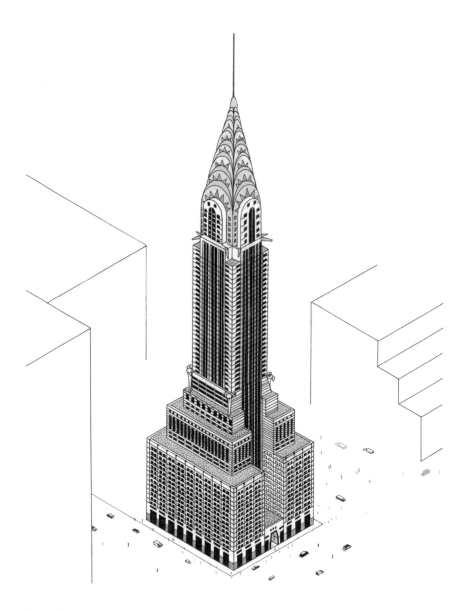

The Chrysler Building, New York (1930)

When the construction of the Empire State Building, which was to reach a height of 1,000 feet (305 meters), was announced around the same time, a competition began to build the world's tallest skyscraper. Van Alen decided to replace the dome he had initially envisioned with a spire, and the Chrysler Building peaked at 1,046 feet (319 meters), making it the tallest skyscraper...

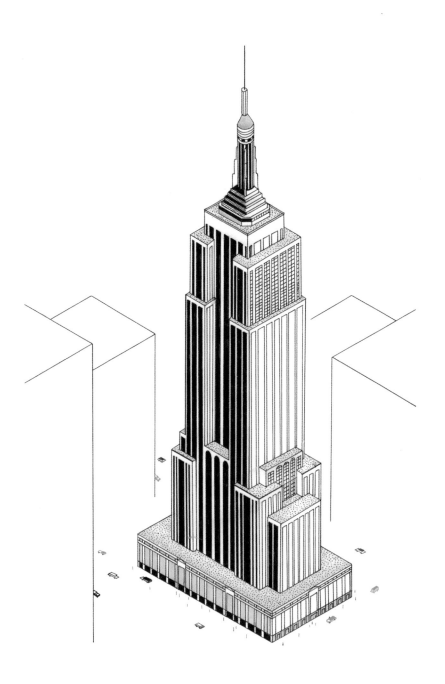

The Empire State Building, New York (1931)

…until the moment a mast for docking airships was added to the top of the Empire State Building, increasing its height to 1,250 feet (381 meters).

The Chrysler Building's record was broken!

The Chrysler Building was the first skyscraper in the art deco style,
which was all the rage at the time.

It's a magnificent building that is tiered and tapered, inspired by
the Babylonian ziggurats.* Its iron framework is entirely covered with
glazed brick.

* Pyramids with sides in the form of steps

The spire, also made of iron, resembles a stack of crowns and is easily recognizable from afar.

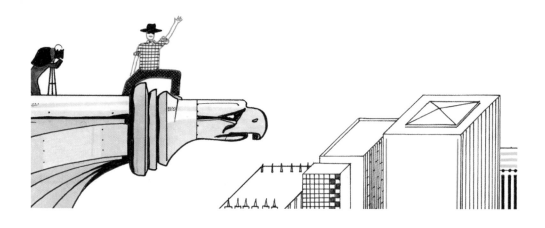

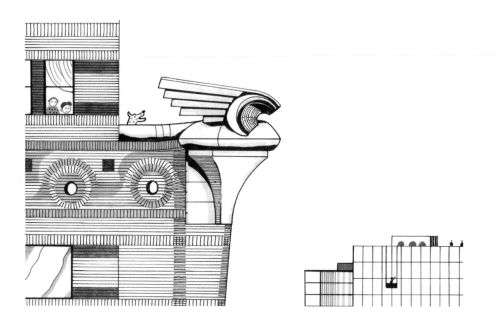

The building is dotted with oversized automobile hubcaps.

The ground floor once served as a display area for beautiful cars.
Visitors enter through a grand lobby decorated with colored marble.

1958
THE SEAGRAM BUILDING

MIES VAN DER ROHE

A SIMPLE AND ELEGANT TOWER

---

515 FEET (157 METERS)

After heading the famous Bauhaus design school in Berlin, architect Ludwig Mies van der Rohe (1886–1969) fled Nazi Germany in 1938 and settled in the United States, becoming the director of Chicago's Illinois Institute of Technology.

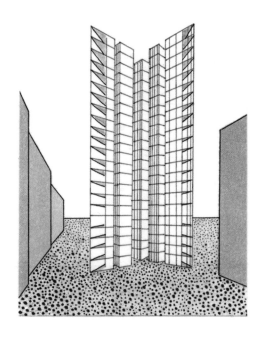

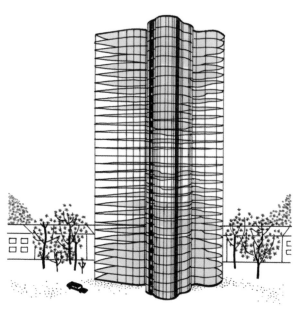

He discovered Chicago's magnificent buildings and befriended
developer Herbert Greenwald. Their work together allowed
the architect to build the glass towers that he had imagined in
the 1920s.

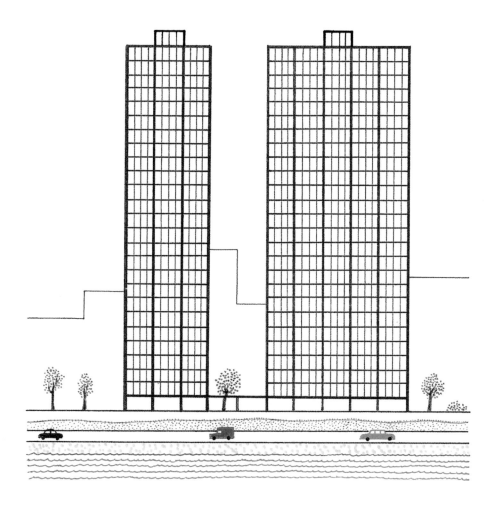

Benefiting from American technological advances, Mies developed
an original system for steel-frame construction. The architect
wanted the structural framework of all his buildings to be visible.
His 860–880 Lake Shore Drive apartment buildings in Chicago
(1951) are a good example.

In the mid-1950s, the Seagram Company asked Mies to design a large office building in New York.

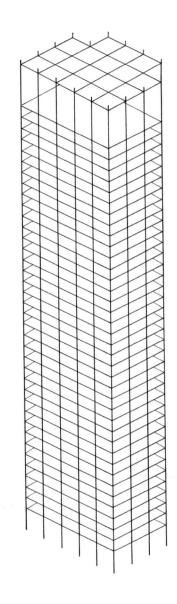

The architect began with a tall steel frame...

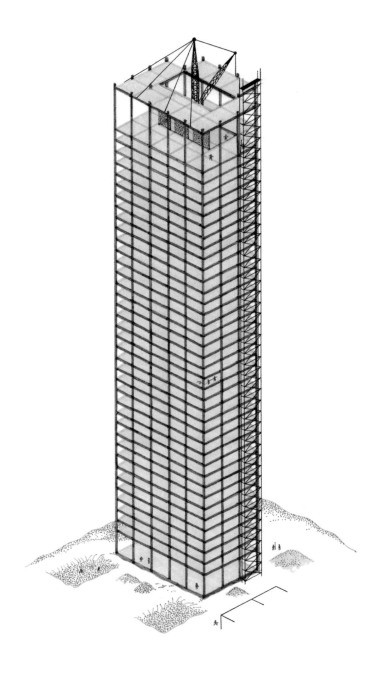

…that was wrapped in concrete to protect it from fire.

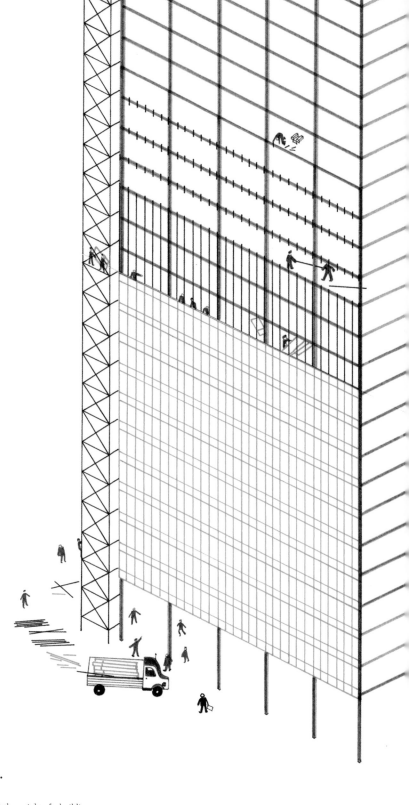

The building was then covered with a glass-and-bronze curtain wall* that emphasized the grid of the skyscraper's underlying structure.

* An outside wall that does not support the weight of a building. Instead, it hangs like a curtain around the building.

Set back from the street and surrounded by a wide plaza that welcomes visitors, the building is splendid.

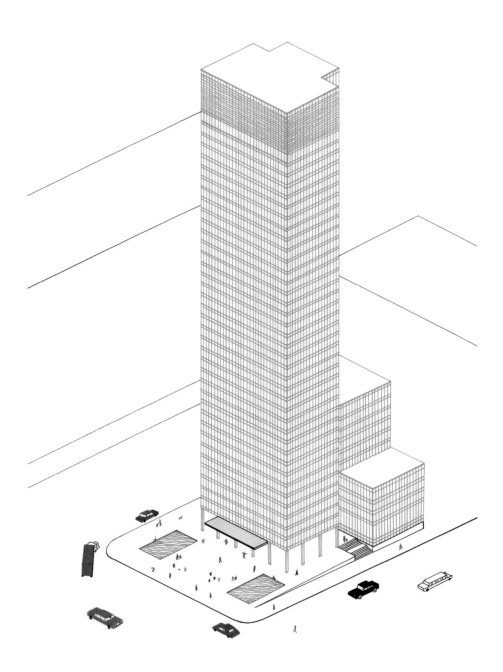

1969
JOHN HANCOCK CENTER

FAZLUR RAHMAN KHAN

A CITY REACHING TO THE SKY

1,127 FEET (344 METERS)

Fazlur Khan (1929–1982) was an Indian engineer who completed his training in applied mechanics and civil engineering in the United States. A partner in the Chicago architectural firm Skidmore, Owings & Merrill, he designed giant skyscrapers, such as the John Hancock Center in Chicago.

The building is constructed as a rigid tube made up of converging metal rods that support all of the floors. The visible steel frame of this monumental obelisk* has a unique appearance.

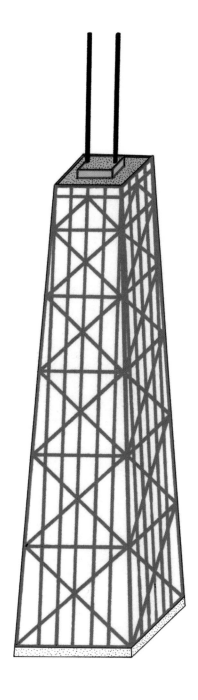

* A four-sided column that gets narrower toward its top

At first, the plan was to build two different towers, one for offices, the other for homes. Because there was not enough space, the buildings were stacked on top of each other, creating a truly vertical city.

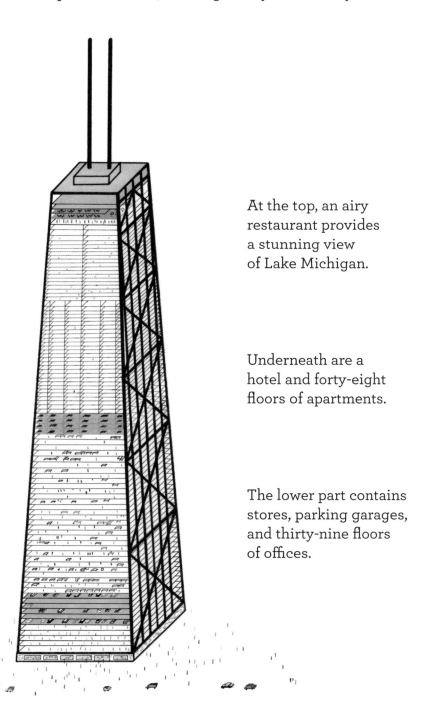

At the top, an airy restaurant provides a stunning view of Lake Michigan.

Underneath are a hotel and forty-eight floors of apartments.

The lower part contains stores, parking garages, and thirty-nine floors of offices.

The building towers over Lake Michigan.

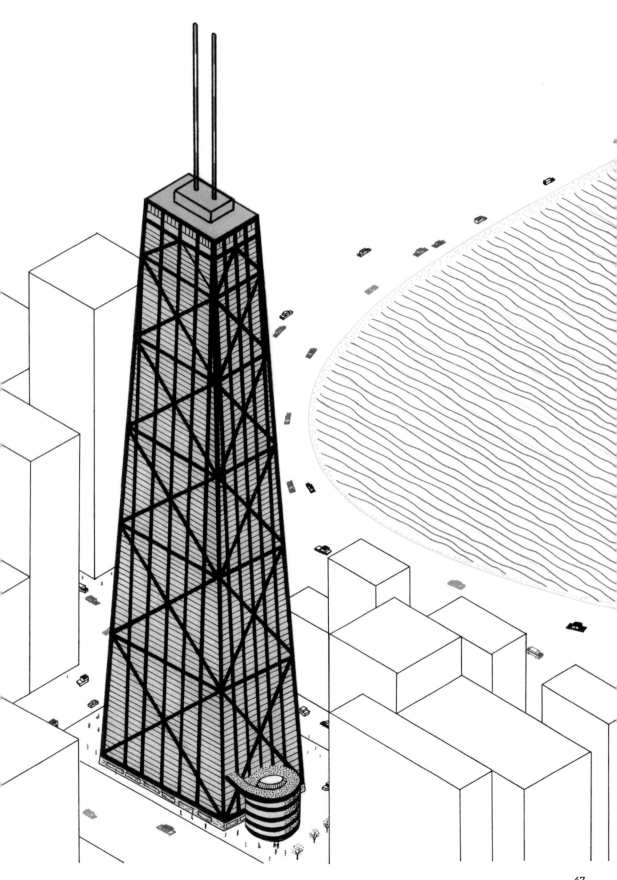

Khan also participated in the design of other projects:

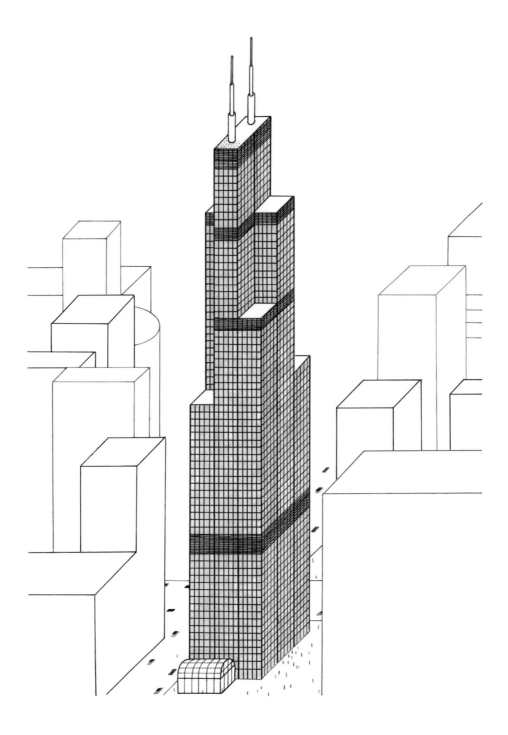

The Sears Tower (today the Willis Tower) in Chicago (1974)

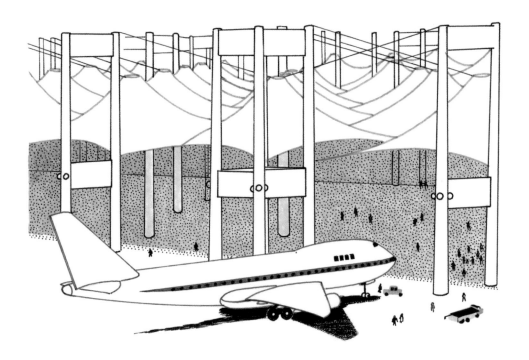

The Hajj Terminal in the Jeddah airport in Saudi Arabia (1981)

1992
MENARA MESINIAGA

KEN YEANG

A BIOCLIMATIC* TOWER

---

206 FEET (63 METERS)

Originally from Malaysia, Ken Yeang
(born in 1948) studied architecture
in London, England. After moving to the
United States, he attended a course taught
by Ian McHarg, a landscape architect,[†]
who encouraged him to develop buildings
for the hot and humid climate of Southeast
Asia. Yeang invented an architecture
that uses natural solutions to manage
heat and humidity.

* Designed to conserve energy though harmony with the environment
† A person who designs outdoor spaces, such as parks or gardens

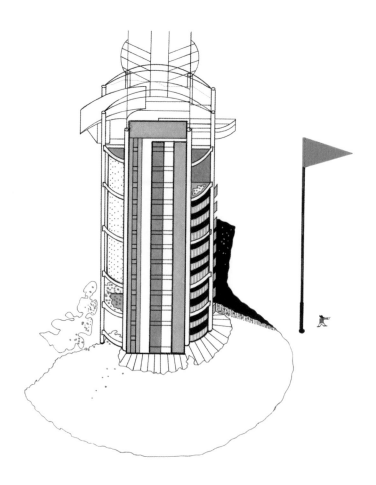

Menara Mesiniaga, IBM's headquarters in Subang Jaya, near Kuala Lumpur in Malaysia, is a monumental iron structure. Yeang, together with T. R. Hamzah, designed its different floors in a variety of shapes. On one side of the building is a series of planted balconies, and external louvers* provide shade from the sun.

On the east side the walls are sealed, protecting rooms from the morning sun.

* Fins that control the movement of air or light in and out of a building

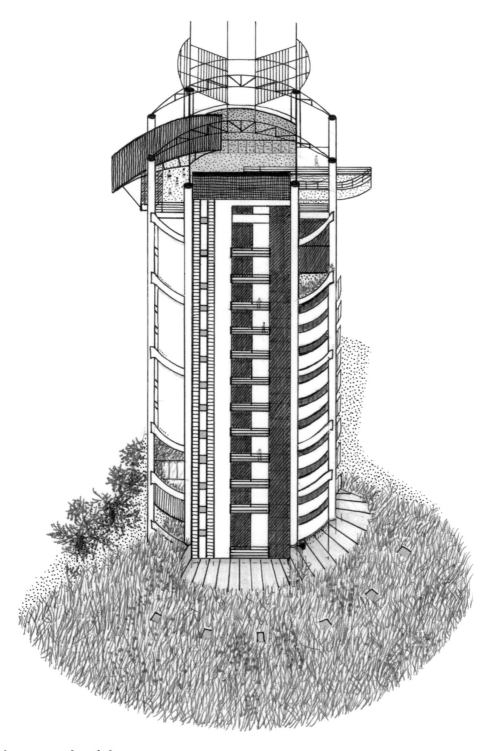

The east side of the tower

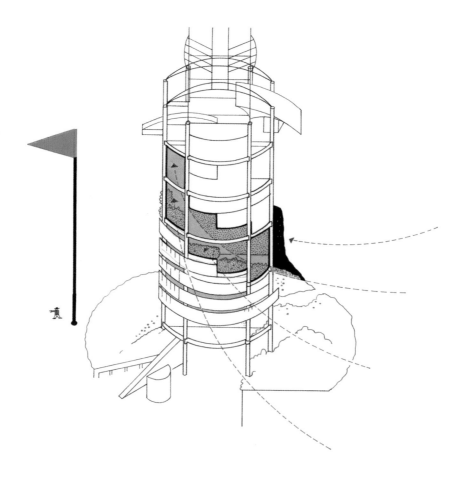

To the west planted balconies spiral up the building, and the offices are spread apart as much as possible to avoid the heat. The wind flows through the tower to cool it naturally. On the roof a sunshield shelters a cooling pool on the top floor.

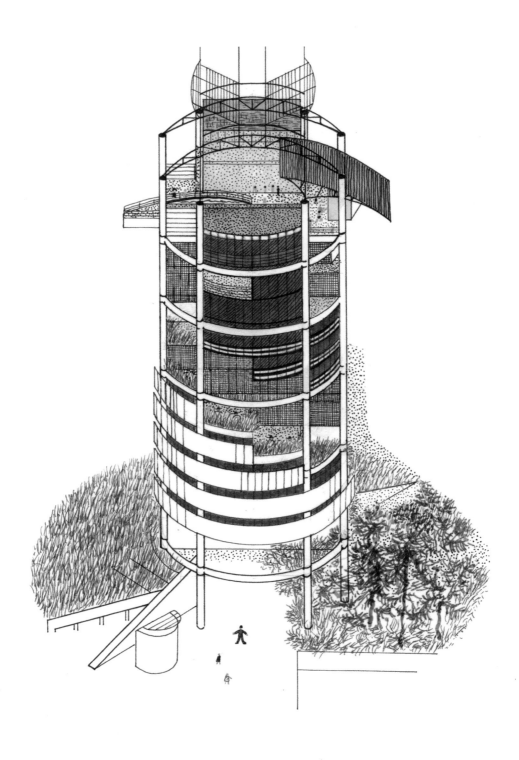

The west side of the tower

Other buildings by Yeang:

The architect's own house, the Roof-Roof House in Kuala Lumpur (1985)

The National Library of Singapore (2005), designed
by T. R. Hamzah and Yeang

Since 2000 Yeang has designed numerous bioclimatic projects that have not yet been built. He envisions plantings on every floor and calls them "hairy office buildings."

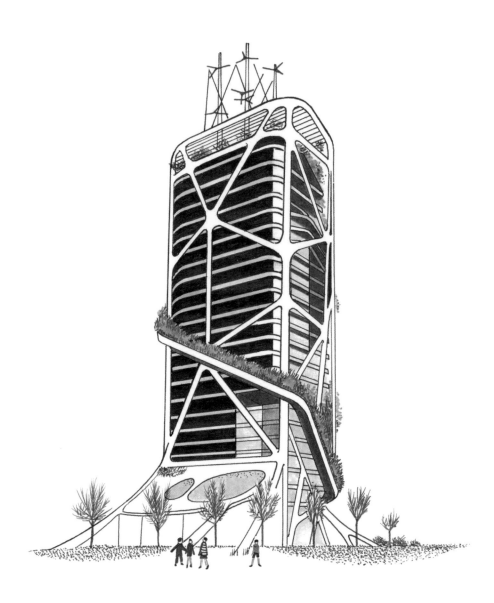

2005
THE TORRE AGBAR

JEAN NOUVEL

A FESTIVE TOWER

466 FEET (142 METERS)

Born in 1945, Jean Nouvel graduated in architecture from the National School of Fine Arts (l'École nationale supérieure des Beaux-Arts) in Paris. He worked as an assistant for groundbreaking architect Claude Parent, then began designing his own projects, which he often carried out in collaboration with artists.

For Nouvel, each project is an opportunity to find new inspiration in a place, history, or culture.

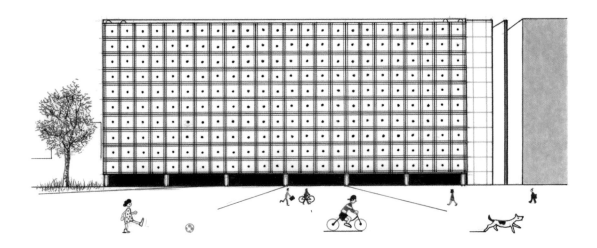

The Arab World Institute in Paris (1987), located between the Jussieu Campus of Pierre and Marie Curie University and the Seine River, relates to the university buildings while standing out through its mashrabiya* facade, whose windows open and close depending on the light.

* A traditional Arabic design in which windows are covered by a patterned screen

For the Tower Without End project, which was ultimately abandoned, a 1,396-foot-tall (400-meter) tube was planned for the business district La Défense, west of Paris. It was designed to blend in with the sky.

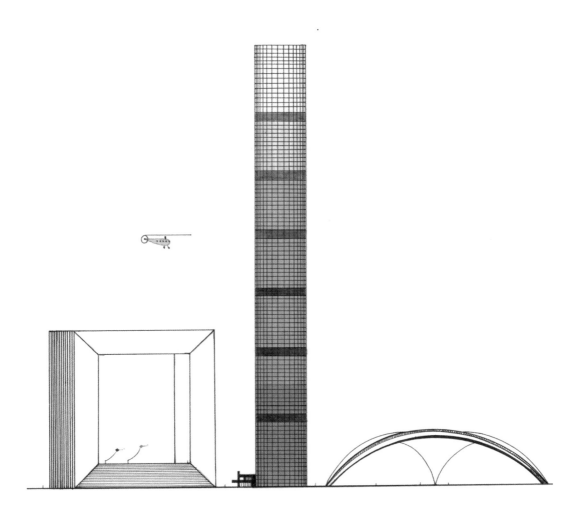

The skyscraper housing the headquarters of the water company Agbar is located in the center of Barcelona, Spain. Nouvel was inspired by the shape of the nearby mountain Montserrat in his design of this egglike concrete tower.

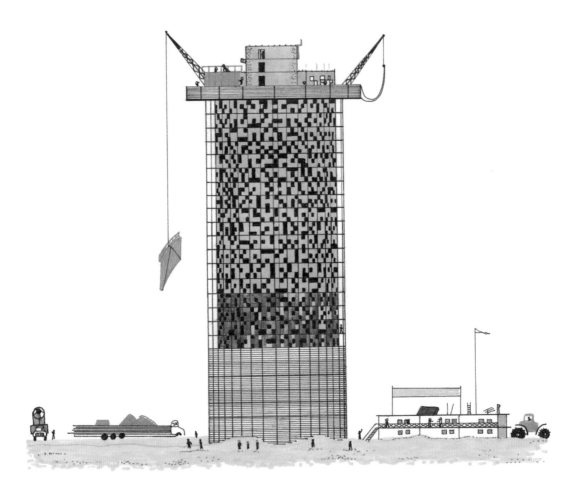

It is composed of an outer ringlike shell and a supporting core, with a concrete crown on top. Here the shell and core rise up and are gradually covered with multicolored, corrugated (wavy) sheet metal and a second skin made of glass strips.

The entire structure is built on ground that is saturated with water, so the foundation had to be dug very deep.

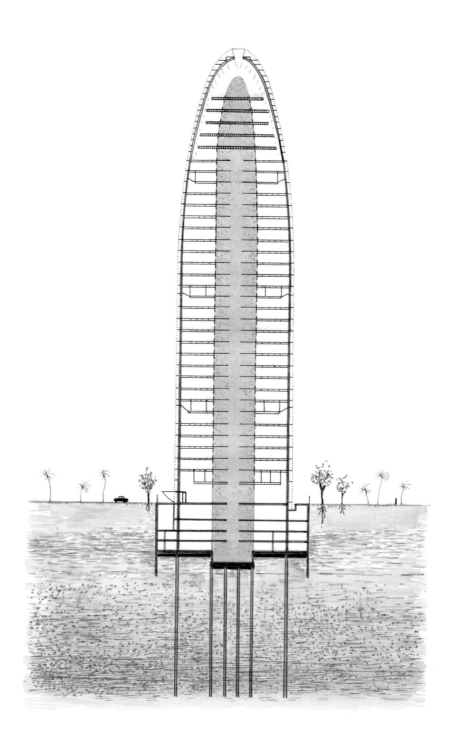

During the day, the tower resembles a frozen water geyser sparkling in the sun.

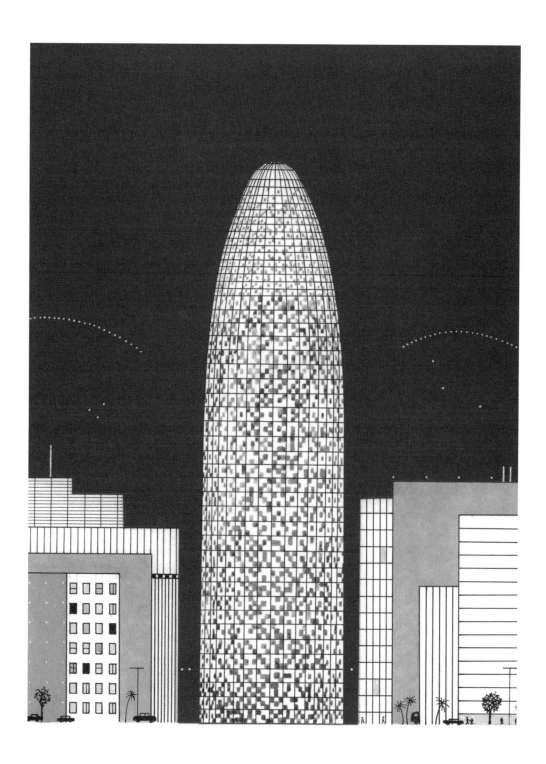

At night, the building is lit up. It has become a landmark, a powerful symbol for the city of Barcelona.

Other towers by Nouvel show how much he has learned about the different cultures of the world:

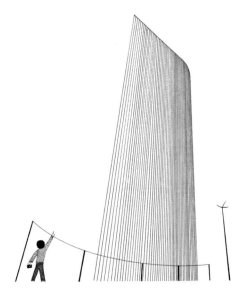

Dentsu Building in Tokyo,
Japan (2002)

Doha Tower in Qatar (2012)

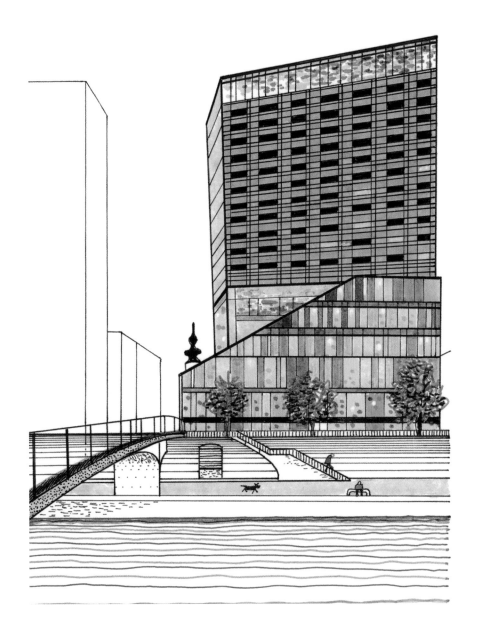

Sofitel Vienna Stephansdom in Vienna, Austria (2010)

2010
BURJ KHALIFA

ADRIAN DEVAUN SMITH

THE TALLEST TOWER IN THE WORLD

2,717 FEET (828 METERS)

Adrian Devaun Smith (born in 1944) studied at the University of Illinois and worked with the engineer Fazlur Khan at the firm Skidmore, Owings & Merrill of Chicago before he established his own firm. He also collaborated with the great Mexican architect Luis Barragán.

A specialist in large buildings, Smith uses the latest technology while remaining mindful of the surrounding urban landscapes.

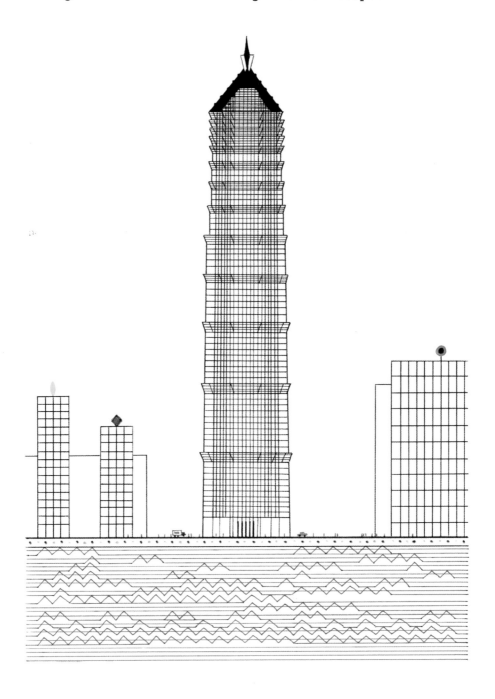

The shape of the Jin Mao Tower in Shanghai, China (1999), is inspired by traditional Chinese forms,…

...and the Trump Tower (2008) blends in with Chicago's skyscrapers.

Dubai's Burj Khalifa tower, designed to dazzle the whole world and rise above its tallest towers—Taiwan's Taipei 101 at 1,666 feet (508 meters) and Kuala Lumpur's Petronas Towers at 1,483 feet (452 meters)— required an enormous construction site on which almost twelve thousand people of more than one hundred nationalities worked. The construction lasted more than six years and resulted in a tower of 2,717 feet (828 meters), with the largest number of floors of any building in the world, the highest-reaching elevator, and the highest observatory ever built, on the 124th floor.

This skyscraper not only contains a large luxury hotel, residences, and offices, but also includes a gigantic sports complex and a mosque.

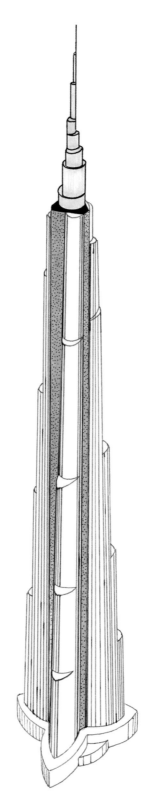

To resist the wind's pressure, Smith designed an original type of structure:

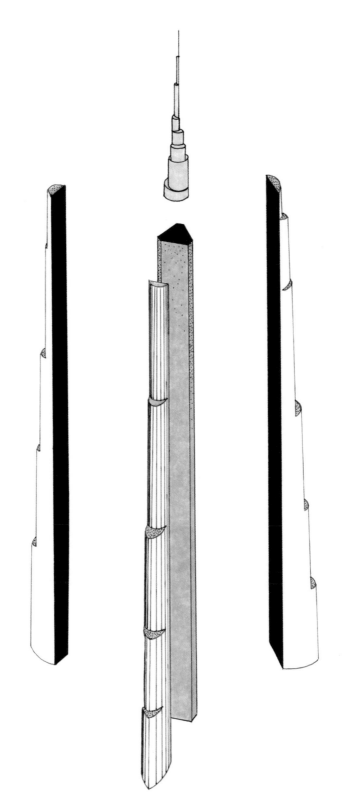

A strong, vertical concrete prism supported by three different parts that form a tripod. Only the very top is made of metal.

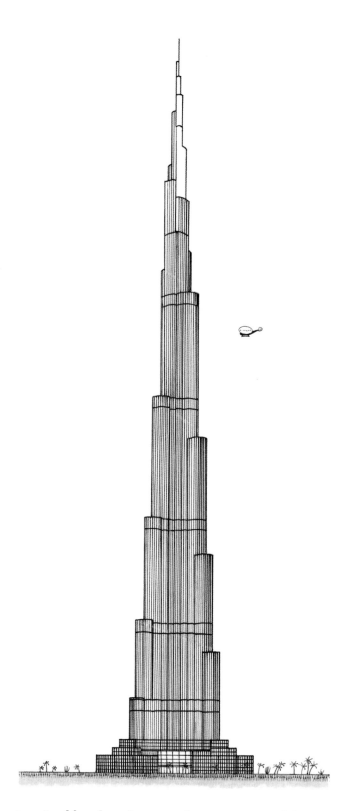

Its form was inspired by the plants and ornaments of the Middle East.
The tower rises in a spiral…

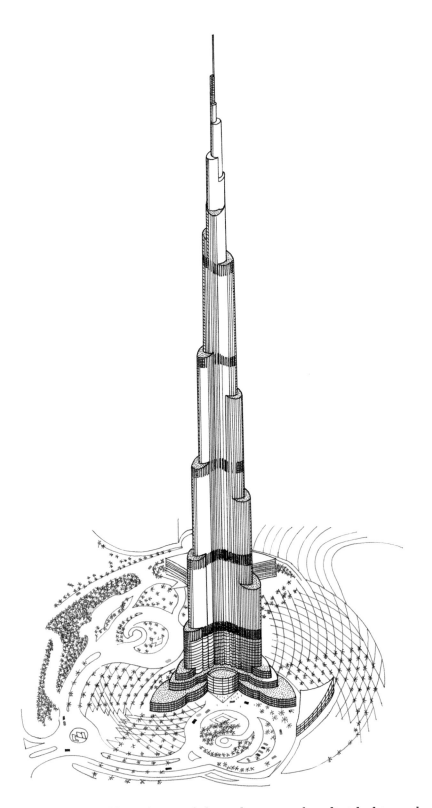

...and is surrounded by a beautiful garden complex divided into three parts, marking the entrances to the hotel, the residences, and the offices.

The architect also worked with Gordon Gill to design a number of bioclimatic projects.

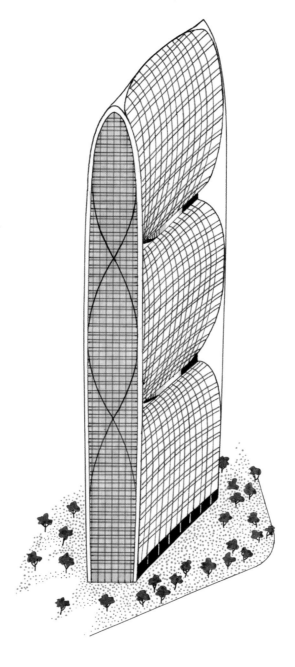

The Pearl River Tower in Guangzhou, China (2013), is an aerodynamic tower.

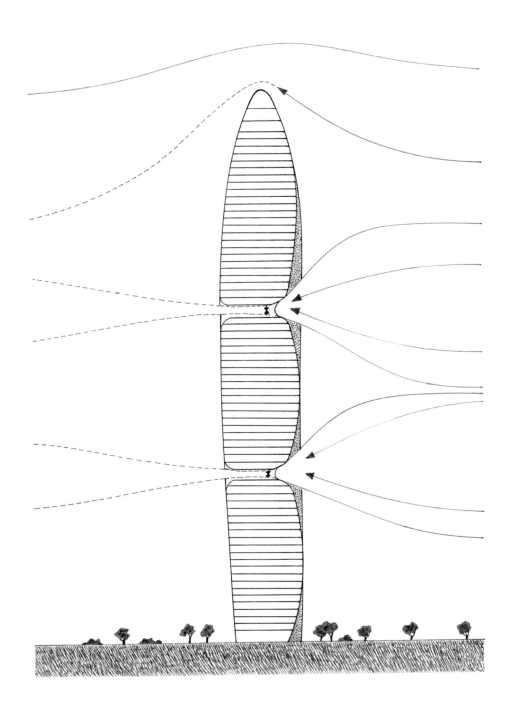

Its rounded facade orients the wind flow toward wind turbines (engines), which produce the tower's electricity.

The imagination of architects has no limits. New technical solutions are constantly being developed to allow the design of new buildings that can provide space for a huge number of people to live and work in the hearts of cities.

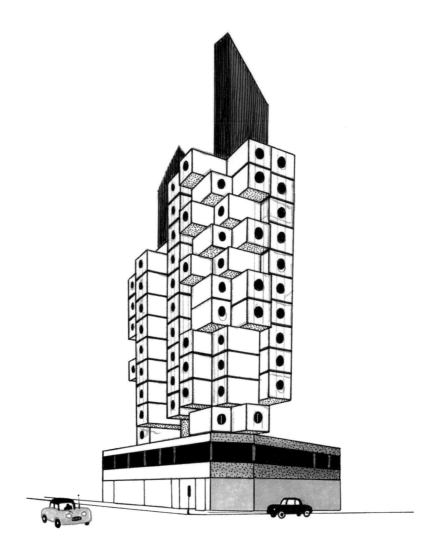

The Nakagin Capsule Tower by Kisho Kurokawa in Tokyo (1971)

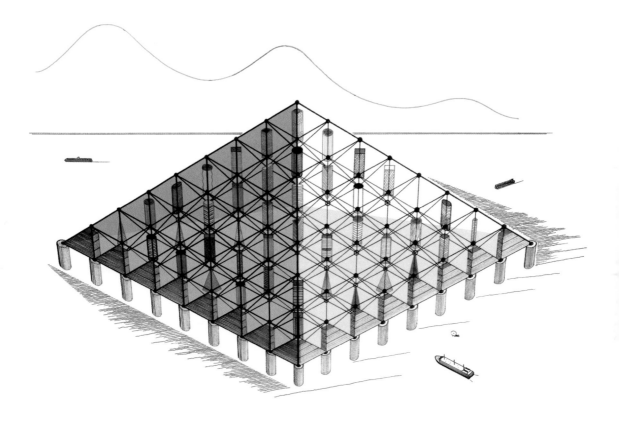

This proposal for the Shimizu TRY 2004 Mega-City Pyramid by the Shimizu Corporation in Japan is currently unbuildable, but eventually materials may be developed that are light and strong enough to make projects like this one possible.

Published in 2014 by
Princeton Architectural Press
37 East Seventh Street
New York, New York 10003

Visit our website at www.papress.com.

First published in France under the title
Toutes les gratte-ciel sont dans la nature
© 2012, hélium/Actes Sud, Paris, France

Copyright English edition
© 2014 Princeton Architectural Press

All rights reserved
Printed and bound in China by C&C Offset
17 16 15 4 3 2

Credits:
The Chrysler Building:
William Van Alen
The Seagram Building:
Mies van der Rohe © ADAGP, Paris, 2014
John Hancock Center:
Fazlur Rahman Khan
Menara Mesiniaga:
Ken Yeang
The Torre Agbar:
Jean Nouvel © ADAGP, Paris, 2014, © L'institut du
Monde Arabe, Architects: Jean Nouvel, Architecture
Studio / ADAGP, Paris, 2014
For the Torre Abgar project:
Ateliers Jean Nouvel & b720—Fermin Vazquez
For the Arab World Institute:
Jean Nouvel, Gilbert Lézénès, Pierre Soria,
Architecture Studio
For The Tower Without End project:
Competition phase: Jean Nouvel & Associates
(Jean Nouvel and Jean-Maec Ibos); Study phase:
Jean Nouvel, Emmanuel Cattani & Associates
For the Dentsu Building project:
Ateliers Jean Nouvel
For the Sofitel Vienna Stephansdom project:
Ateliers Jean Nouvel
Burj Khalifa Tower:
Adrian Devaun Smith

For Princeton Architectural Press:
Project editor: Nicola Brower
Typesetting: Paul Wagner

Special thanks to: Meredith Baber, Sara Bader,
Janet Behning, Megan Carey, Carina Cha,
Andrea Chlad, Barbara Darko, Benjamin English,
Russell Fernandez, Will Foster, Jan Hartman,
Jan Haux, Diane Levinson, Jennifer Lippert,
Katharine Myers, Jaime Nelson, Jay Sacher,
Rob Shaeffer, Sara Stemen, Marielle Suba, and
Joseph Weston of Princeton Architectural Press
—Kevin C. Lippert, publisher

Library of Congress Cataloging-in-Publication Data

Cornille, Didier, 1951-
[Tous les gratte-ciel sont dans la nature. English]
Skyscrapers : who built that? : an introduction to
skyscrapers and their architects / Didier Cornille.
— First edition.
     pages   cm
«First published in France under the title Toutes les
gratte-ciel sont dans la nature (c) 2012, Hélium, Paris,
France.»
ISBN 978-1-61689-270-8 (alk. paper)
1. Skyscrapers—Juvenile literature. I. Cornille,
Didier, 1951- Tous les gratte-ciel sont dans la nature.
Translation of: II. Title.
NA6230.C6713 2014
720'.483—dc23
              2014004388